FACING
THE CROSS
FINDING OURSELVES

Tony Kidd

6 Bible studies for individuals or groups
A Lent Resource

Scripture Union

Scripture Union, 207–209 Queensway, Bletchley, MK2 2EB, England.
Email: info@scriptureunion.org.uk
Web site: www.scriptureunion.org.uk

British Library Cataloguing-in-Publication Data
A catalogue record for this book is available from the British Library.

Cover design by Grax Design.
Illustrations by Helen Gale.
Printed and bound in Great Britain by Creative Print and Design (Wales), Ebbw Vale.

FACING
THE CROSS
FINDING OURSELVES

CONTENTS

PREFACE

Recently, at a service for the 'installation and induction' of a vicar, a man who had been persuaded to accompany his churchgoing wife was heard to remark that the service was 'a load of out-of-date mumbo-jumbo'. He asserted that even the service name sounded more like 'a programme for putting in a warm-air heating system than anything to do with God'. Increasingly, religious language and ritual presents a problem for many people wanting to explore the purpose and meaning of life, who accept that life does have a spiritual dimension but see organised religion as 'hoop-jumping' religiosity rather than spiritual quest.

These days, spiritual navigators, especially those from the developed world, may well sail along lanes far removed from those explored by their predecessors. Crystals, aromatherapy, tai chi, transcendental meditation, eastern religions – all have attracted increased interest. Paganism and ethnic religions have also received attention from those hoping to rediscover an ancient understanding of the world which, they think, may have come from a much greater awareness and respect for it than is shown today. This way of searching for truth is echoed in the emerging scientific understanding of our universe, in which scientists have been establishing just how close, at the deepest level, seems to be the relationship between all parts of the world, and that includes us.

Elsewhere in human society, the search goes on for ideal role models. The old gods are dead and humankind has taken their place. The spirit of the age now expresses itself in fashion, labels, shopping (Tesco ergo sum), style, image, and all the gurus, gods and guides that go with them. Such a spirit spills over into sport, entertainment, even politics. Edges become blurred and distinctions unclear. For people attracted to this aspect of our culture, human experience becomes all absorbing, and spirituality is seen as a continuous journey towards self-discovery initiated by the imitation of the lifestyles and choices of the stars, personalities and celebrities promoted by the media. Truth relates more to experiencing the moment, through which is experienced 'the beyond'. Connectedness with our emotions, it is believed, is strengthened by our oneness with those of like mind. It is accepted that many who follow this path do not actually go on to achieve any particular goal.

This diversity of approaches, some of which, in many parts of the world, are the result of greater affluence, technological advances and mass communication, has facilitated a growing awareness and prompted a reaction. Maybe God is not dead after all. Perhaps it is just that our way of approaching God has caused us to lose sight of the fundamental truths which lie buried beneath the layers of dogma, regulation and jargon that all human institutions produce, not least religious ones.

From an appraisal of the current scene emerge at least three points of interest. First, there is undoubtedly a growing spiritual awareness pervading much of secular society. Secondly, meditation and prayer, even if the latter is not referred to as often as the former, are commonly practised by those who would not choose to classify themselves as religious or describe what they are doing in those terms. Thirdly, many are searching for a focal point and/or guide or guru, whether it be the Beatles, the players for the England football team, someone reading Maester Eckhart or Thomas Merton for the first time, or travellers looking to discover the real significance of ancient stones or pyramids.

The Christian contribution steadfastly remains that of Jesus of Nazareth as role model and the Holy Spirit as guide. In these six studies, the exploration is not of the more comfortable aspects of human experience but, rather, those that challenge us. Perhaps some of those who rejected the 'hoop-jumping' referred to earlier will, nevertheless, find these six steps helpful in their own journey.

Tony Kidd

INTRODUCTION

The challenge of the cross is that so often it points in a fundamentally different direction from that advocated by those who are, or who seem to be, successful in the world around us. It is not the cross in isolation which does this – after all, Good Friday was just one day in Jesus' life. However, the cross is at the heart of the journey to salvation which Jesus maps out for us.

In his invitation to us to follow in his footsteps, he challenges us to be prepared to examine ourselves, our motives and our standards. He asks us to be prepared to be unpopular, to face hardships, to swim against the tide of worldly opinion and to be able to cope with ridicule. His is not an easy way, but he promises us that at the end of it lies fulfilment in eternity for the relationship we develop with him as we travel through the here and now.

This course has been written primarily for use by groups, although it may also be helpful to individuals. A group of six to ten people is ideal. Group members may like to appoint a leader, or take it in turns over the six weeks to be responsible for facilitating the group and keeping time. Allow between one-and-a-half and two hours for each session. Suggested timings for the specific sections are:

Way in.......10–15 minutes	Response...15–20 minutes
Bible..........20–30 minutes	Prayer ....10–20 minutes
Life..............5–10 minutes	

Included are suggestions for songs that reflect the theme for each session and these can be found in *Mission Praise* (MP), *Songs of Fellowship* (SOF) and *The Source* (TS). There are also suggestions for music to be played when leading into times of prayer or during the meditations.

The Bible passages are from *New Revised Standard Version* (NRSV) and are printed in full. The group may prefer to read these in silence. Alternatively:

- One person reads the passage aloud while the others listen.

- Two or three people read alternate verses.

- One person takes the role of narrator while others read any dialogue.

The meditations may be approached in three ways:

- You may like to read them on your own silently or, if no one else is near, out loud.

- If you are in a group, one person could read the meditation to the others. The passage should be read slowly, with pauses at appropriate points to allow time for people to take in the atmosphere and bring their imaginations into play.

- If the person reading to the group is feeling fairly confident, they might use the meditation as a basis for painting their own picture of the scene, pausing after each line to interject imagery or description.

An illustration appears near each meditation to provide a focus, but you may like to bring to the session an appropriate object such as a spray of leaves or flowers, a cross or a candle. Other pictures, either photographs or prints of paintings, can be used. Be creative in thinking up ways to add interest and variety.

NOTE

- At times of sharing, no one should feel obliged to say more than they want to, and individual privacy must always be respected. As a group, be sensitive to the possibility that some members may find parts of the sessions difficult. Providing support in such circumstances could be helpful.

- The text contains points at which silence can be used. Some may find silence uncomfortable, so offer reassurance beforehand. Let people know how long the silence will last, and that they can use it for quiet prayer, to unburden themselves from the pressures of the day, or simply to be still before God.

The pattern of prayer on pages 23–24 is designed for use each day during the course, and may be adapted to suit personal taste and practice. The daily readings form a natural part of the pattern of prayer. The following are the readings for the three days before the first meeting and during the meeting itself (which is marked ◆):

Preparation	Day 1	Matthew 25:14–30, The trustworthy slave
	Day 2	Matthew 25:31–46, Righteousness and eternal life
	Day 3	Hebrews 12:1–11, God's children
◆ Meeting	Day 4	Matthew 5:1–12, Those who are blessed

1 FACING THE CHALLENGE OF THE CROSS

Aim: to consider how we face up to the challenges with which Jesus confronts us.

WAY IN

Talk with another person in the group about any challenge to your beliefs, values or standards, which you have had to face either personally or alongside someone else you care about. Commit to prayer any issues raised during your conversation.

Songs to sing
A new commandment, SOF22, MP1.
Father, I place into your hands, SOF97, MP133, TS97.
Fight the good fight, SOF107, MP143.
Jesus shall reign, SOF301, MP379.
Just as I am, SOF316, MP396, TS306.
Living under the shadow of his wing, SOF346, MP423, TS323.
Make way, make way, SOF384, MP457, TS349.
Such love, SOF514, MP619, TS465.
There's a quiet understanding, SOF546, MP678.

Music to listen to
Telemann: Trumpet Concerto in D major (Adagio), from *Adagio 2*.

'Sanctus' (based on a canon by Pachabel), from *Libera*.
Enya: 'The Memory of Trees', from *The Memory of Trees*.

Read Matthew 5:1–12; Those who are blessed

When Jesus saw the crowds, he went up the mountain; and after he sat down, his disciples came to him. Then he began to speak, and taught them, saying:

'Blessed are the poor in spirit, for theirs is the kingdom of heaven.

'Blessed are those who mourn, for they will be comforted.

'Blessed are the meek, for they will inherit the earth.

'Blessed are those who hunger and thirst for righteousness, for they will be filled.

'Blessed are the merciful, for they will receive mercy.

'Blessed are the pure in heart, for they will see God.

'Blessed are the peacemakers, for they will be called children of God.

'Blessed are those who are persecuted for righteousness' sake, for theirs is the kingdom of heaven.

'Blessed are you when people revile you and persecute you and utter all kinds of evil against you falsely on my account. Rejoice and be glad, for your reward is great in heaven, for in the same way they persecuted the prophets who were before you.'

Jesus was aware from the outset of his ministry that his message would not be popular with everyone who heard it. However, he did not dilute what he had to say even though it led to the threat of physical violence (Luke 4:24–30). He insisted that people look at themselves and the reality of their conduct and beliefs, not just its appearance (Luke 5:27–32). He called upon his audience not merely to observe the law, but to understand what that law ought to mean for them in their daily lives, demanding that they let this understanding flow outward in loving action (Matt 25:37–40). This he termed 'righteousness'.

Jesus was also prepared to challenge the religious hierarchy, which was the establishment of his day. In uncompromising terms, he confronted them with their hypocrisy (Luke 11:37–43).

In his challenge to the disciples and to all who came to listen to him (Matt 5:10–12), Jesus made it clear that following in his footsteps would involve unpopularity on such a scale that it would lead to rejection, perhaps even death. Nevertheless, he maintained that such a price was worth paying in the name of love (John 15:12–13).

If we are prepared to make sacrifices for those we love, following Jesus' example, then he promises us that our joy will become complete.

Discussion
As a group, consider and then discuss how, in today's world, we can recognise 'righteousness' and respond to 'persecution'.

LIFE

In facing the challenge of Jesus' teaching and his conduct, we must be prepared to face the cross itself. What effect do you think doing this would have on your relationship with...

    1) Jesus

2) people with whom you work or are in fellowship?

3) those to whom you are closest?

What have you discovered about yourself from that experience, and is there anything you need to do as a result?

RESPONSE

Discuss together any responses to the questions in the 'Life' section which have troubled, surprised or encouraged you. Pray for anyone you know who is facing a difficult or uncertain future.

MEDITATION

The Challenge

They say I'm stupid to be religious.
They say I'm no better than they are, worse in fact.
They say, 'Look at what religious people have done –
all those wars, all that torture and cruelty.'
They say church is boring and looks down its nose at people.
They say they have fun and it never did anybody any harm.
There's nothing wrong with money
and the poor have always been with us.
They say people like me are just jealous
of people with money, clothes and cars,
people who can afford nice things.

continued >>>

Am I like that? How can I tell?
I sometimes think it would be so much easier
just to fit in, to join,
to go where they go, to wear and enjoy
whatever and wherever.
I could pretend, say it's alright and not make a fuss.
After all, they're nice people
and think they don't hurt anyone.

But that's the point, isn't it?
That's how Jesus came to die.
Those who shouted, 'Hosanna',
a week later shouted, 'Crucify',
because the fashion changed.

It's hard being a believer in Jesus,
but then they hated him first.

Praise

Leader:	The Lord calls his servants.
All:	**We will fear no evil.**
Leader:	The Lord calls the chosen.
All:	**We will not be rejected.**
Leader:	The Lord upholds with righteousness.
All:	**The Lord is our strength and helper.**

(Based on Isaiah 41:8–10)

READINGS FOR THE WEEK

1 Facing the challenge of the cross

Reflection	Day 5	Matthew 10:1–16, Sending the disciples
	Day 6	Matthew 10:17–31, Warning the disciples
	Day 7	Matthew 10:32–42, Taking up the cross

2 Facing injustice

Preparation	Day 1	Psalm 64:1–10, The scheming of evildoers
	Day 2	Isaiah 58:1–14, The bonds of injustice
	Day 3	Habakkuk 1:1–4, The persistence of the wicked
◆ Meeting	Day 4	Matthew 12:22–28; 26:57–60; Luke 23:39–43, False accusations

PATTERN OF PRAYER

You may like to use this pattern as a basis for your daily prayers during the course.

Praise and thanksgiving
Spend a few moments thinking of the things you want to thank God for, then offer them up to him in praise.

> I will praise the greatness of my God.
> I will praise his perfect works.
> I will praise my God, my Rock and my Salvation.
>
> *(Based on Deuteronomy 32:3–4)*

Confession
Spend a few moments thinking of things you need to confess, asking for forgiveness.

> Turn to the Lord our God
> Who pardons and forgives.
> Turn to the Lord our God
> Who loves to show compassion.
> Turn to the Lord our God
> Who delights in being merciful.
>
> *(Based on Micah 7:18–20)*

Bible

On each day when you are preparing for the next session, read the Bible passage and spend time reflecting on it, making notes of any feelings you experience.   **OR**

On each day when you are reflecting on the last session, re-read the key Bible passage (◆) for the session and make notes of any new thoughts or feelings you have.   **THEN**

Use the reading for the day, or the meditation for the week to come, and be still before God.

Intercession

Bring to God:

- any people or situations that you feel need his love.
- the other members of the group.
- your own needs.

The Lord's Prayer
Our Father in heaven,
Hallowed be your name.
Your kingdom come,
your will be done on earth as it is in heaven.
Give us today our daily bread.
Forgive us our sins
as we forgive those who sin against us.
Lead us not into temptation
but deliver us from evil.
For the kingdom, the power and
the glory are yours
now and forever. Amen.

In closing

Lord, let me go out in the peace of Jesus Christ.
In his name I ask it. Amen.

_2_ FACING INJUSTICE

Aim: to consider how Jesus dealt with injustice and how his example can help us.

WAY IN

Have you ever had to face injustice personally or alongside someone you care about? Discuss this with another member of the group for a few minutes, then pray about the issues raised.

Songs to sing
Ascribe greatness, SOF26, MP40, TS25.
Come and praise the living God, SOF66, MP84.
God forgave my sin, SOF129, MP181, TS123.
He walked where I walk, SOF172, MP221, TS168.
In heavenly armour, SOF237, MP639, TS228.
Lord, we long for you, SOF365, MP448, TS337.
Man of sorrows, SOF385, MP458, TS350.
One shall tell another, SOF439, MP541, TS406.
Reconciled, I'm reconciled, SOF477, MP568.
Who can sound the depth of sorrow, SOF604, MP766, TS579.

Music to listen to
Bach: Concerto for violin and oboe in C minor (Adagio), from *Adagio 2*.
'Te lucis' (based on a canon by Tallis), from *Libera*.
Enya: 'From where I am', from *The Memory of Trees*.

Read Matthew 12:22–28; 26:57–60; Luke 23:39–43; False accusations

Then they brought to him a demoniac who was blind and mute; and he cured him, so that the one who had been mute could speak and see. All the crowds were amazed and said, 'Can this be the Son of David?' But when the Pharisees heard it, they said, 'It is only by Beelzebub, the ruler of the demons, that this fellow casts out the demons.' He knew what they were thinking and said to them, 'Every kingdom divided against itself is laid waste, and no city or house divided against itself will stand. If Satan casts out Satan, he is divided against himself; how then will his kingdom stand? If I cast out demons by Beelzebub, by whom do your own exorcists cast them out? Therefore they will be your judges. But if it is by the Spirit of God that I cast out demons, then the kingdom of God has come to you.'

Those who had arrested Jesus took him to Caiaphas the high priest, in whose house the scribes and the elders had gathered. But Peter was following him at a distance, as far as the courtyard of the high priest; and going inside, he sat with the guards in order to see how this would end. Now the chief priests and the whole council were looking for false testimony against Jesus so that they might put him to death, but they found none, though many false witnesses came forward.

> One of the criminals who were hanged there kept deriding him and saying, 'Are you not the Messiah? Save yourself and us!' But the other rebuked him, saying, 'Do you not fear God, since you are under the same sentence of condemnation? And we indeed have been condemned justly, for we are getting what we deserve for our deeds, but this man has done nothing wrong.' Then he said, 'Jesus, remember me when you come into your kingdom.' He replied, 'Truly I tell you, today you will be with me in Paradise.'

As Jesus' ministry became more widely known, the authorities became increasingly agitated about his popularity and impact. They had to find plausible reasons for Jesus' evident success in healing, for example. They needed to counteract what they regarded as a threat to their authority. So it came to pass that the 'spin doctors' of Jesus' time got to work in order to discredit him, and truth became their first casualty. When, however, the Pharisees suggested that Jesus' ability to cast out demons might be the work of Beelzebub, Jesus demolished their argument swiftly and easily (Matt 12:22–28). When he appeared before the Sanhedrin, a string of false witnesses were produced to discredit him, but without success. Eventually it was only when Jesus restored the integrity of truth and chose to confess who he was, that they were able to condemn him. Truth, not the lies of his accusers, brought about his death, and it is the injustice of this which confronts us now (Matt 26:64).

One person who stood firm in the face of pressure from the temple authorities to lie, was the man who had been blind from birth (John 9:1–41). He bore witness to the truth (vs 30–33) and would not be shaken from it, even though he was thrown out of the synagogue. One of the dying thieves also recognised the injustice of Jesus' crucifixion, and saved his own soul as a result. In looking at ourselves, how do we cope with injustice when it comes our way?

Discussion

Injustice has been with us from the earliest times. It was faced by Jesus and by the prophets before him, and by Jews and many others in the present day. As a group, consider and then discuss how we deal with injustice as a church or individual. Is there more we could do to counteract the effects of injustice?

LIFE

Thinking about the injustice you have encountered, what effect has it had on your relationship with...

1) Jesus?

2) people with whom you work or are in fellowship?

3) those to whom you are closest?

4) What have you discovered about yourself from that experience, and is there anything you need to do as a result?

RESPONSE

Discuss together any responses to the questions in the 'Life' section which have troubled or encouraged you. Pray for anyone who has recently suffered or who is now facing injustice.

MEDITATION

Facing personal injustice

It wasn't me, I wasn't there.
Ask anyone, they'll tell you.

But they don't.
Instead they just melt away,
become blind and deaf; saw nothing, heard less.

Was it at school, when you were declared guilty
and couldn't prove your innocence?
Was it the car that gave no signals, had no lights
and nobody remembered and you just happened to follow,
seeing the danger too late?
Why was it your brother or sister
always had an excuse that was accepted, and you never did?

The bus can't take any more.
The last ticket has just been sold.
We would have promoted you,
but we knew you'd understand.
There'll be another chance – but there never is.
Suppose that this is your opportunity,
this is why you were born?
What if you don't condemn those who choose
to be blind and deaf,
but accept them as they are and move on?
There is another place where the injustice
we suffer now is put into perspective.

If only we could learn acceptance rather than retaliation.
And, by the way, have *you* always seen, heard and spoken up?

Praise

Leader:	The Lord will establish justice.
All:	**Our hope is in the Lord.**
Leader:	The Lord will never falter.
All:	**Our hope is in the Lord.**
Leader:	He will not be discouraged.
All:	**Justice will come to the nations.**

(Based on Isaiah 42:3–4)

READINGS FOR THE WEEK

2 Facing injustice

Reflection	Day 5	Psalm 43:1–5, God's vindication
	Day 6	Acts 6:8–15, The power of grace
	Day 7	Acts 7:48–60, Grace victorious

3 Facing disloyalty and desertion

Preparation	Day 1	Luke 22:1–6, Blood money
	Day 2	Mark 14:43–52, Betrayal complete
	Day 3	Mark 15:33–37, The loneliness of obedience
◆ Meeting	Day 4	Matthew 26:69–75, Denial

3 FACING DISLOYALTY AND DESERTION

Aim: using Jesus' example to explore how we cope with disloyalty and desertion.

WAY IN

Talk for a few minutes with your neighbour about any instance of disloyalty or desertion by family, friend or colleagues you have had to face either personally or alongside someone else you care about. Pray together about the matters you have discussed.

Songs to sing
Behold the darkness, SOF38, MP36.
Come, let us sing of a wonderful love, SOF72, MP94.
Have thine own way, Lord, SOF156, MP212.
How I love you, SOF190, MP246.
I heard the voice of Jesus say, SOF215, MP275, TS206.
Jesus, lover of my soul, SOF297, MP372, TS290.
Meekness and majesty, SOF390, MP465, TS353.
My Lord, what love is this, SOF398, MP476, TS370.
When we walk with the Lord, SOF599, MP760.

Music to listen to
Schubert: String quintet in C major (Adagio), from *Adagio 2*.
'Agnus dei', from *Libera*.
Enya: 'Once you had gold', from *The Memory of Trees*.

Read Matthew 26:69–75; Denial

Now Peter was sitting outside in the courtyard. A servant-girl came to him and said, 'You also were with Jesus the Galilean.' But he denied it before all of them, saying, 'I do not know what you are talking about.' When he went out to the porch, another servant-girl saw him, and she said to the bystanders, 'This man was with Jesus of Nazareth.' Again he denied it with an oath, 'I do not know the man.' After a little while the bystanders came up and said to Peter, 'Certainly you are also one of them, for your accent betrays you.' Then he began to curse, and he swore an oath, 'I do not know the man!' At that moment the cock crowed. Then Peter remembered what Jesus had said: 'Before the cock crows, you will deny me three times.' And he went out and wept bitterly.

As the authorities closed in on him, Jesus had some bitter pills to swallow. Judas, one of the twelve people closest to him, agreed to betray him (Matt 26:14–16). Then another, Peter, denied that he knew him. Although Jesus had foreseen this (Mark 14:27–30), the reality of it, following as it did hard on the heels of the fleeing disciples, must have been hard to bear.

When it came to it and he had been crucified, there, a little way off from the place of execution, stood just one disciple. And it was to him, John, that Jesus entrusted the care of his mother. Standing with John and Mary were a few women –

they were all that remained of Jesus' support (John 19:25–27).

The scene at Golgotha was a stark contrast to the mass of people who had welcomed Jesus to Jerusalem just a week before (Mark 11:1–11). This teaches us just how fickle the apparent solidarity of the crowd can be. It builds up its idols and, just as quickly, can destroy them. The biographies of many once-famous people reveal how they were in demand for a while, then someone more interesting came along and they were dropped. God is not deceived by the way the world deals with popularity, and neither should we be (Psalm 78:36–37).

Discussion

How important is popularity to you? How do you handle it when those you thought you could rely on let you down? As a group, think about the example of Jesus and then discuss how we might handle the disloyalty or the desertion of a friend or colleague.

LIFE

In facing disloyalty or desertion, what effect has it had on your relationship with…

1) Jesus?

2) people with whom you work or are in fellowship?

3) those to whom you are closest?

4) What have you discovered about yourself from that experience, and is there anything you need to do as a result?

RESPONSE

Discuss together any responses to the questions in the 'Life' section which have troubled, surprised or encouraged you. Pray for anyone who has recently suffered or who is now facing disloyalty or loss.

MEDITATION

Disloyalty

I will never stand against you.
You will have my full support.
I will always be behind you, come what may.
We will always work together.
You will always have my vote.
I will never undermine or block your way.

But, of course, if others ask me
to present a different view
and to lead a power group that's in revolt,
I'll examine my position
and consider where I stand,
then strike you down and say it's all your fault.

For relationships are like that –
easy come and easy go.
They are only momentary, not for life.
And so nothing lasts forever,
we must all be moving on
and soon it will be my turn for the knife.

But now I start to wonder
as I think about it all,

continued >>>

having gained control with guile and with verve;
as I gaze into the mirror
count the lines and see the scars,
who was it then I thought I meant to serve?

Praise

Leader:	The Lord remains silent.
All:	**He is rejected by us.**
Leader:	The Lord is despised and sorrowful.
All:	**He is rejected by us.**
Leader:	The Lord is not esteemed.
All:	**Yet we believe his message.**

(Based on Isaiah 53:1–3)

READINGS FOR THE WEEK

3 Facing disloyalty and desertion

Reflection	Day 5	John 20:10–18, Loyalty rewarded
	Day 6	John 20:19–23, Desertion forgiven
	Day 7	John 21:15–19, Denial forgiven

4 Facing pain and violence

Preparation	Day 1	Psalm 22:1–24, Preparing to face pain
	Day 2	John 18:1–11, Violence to others rebuked
	Day 3	John 18:19–24, Pointless violence
◆ Meeting	Day 4	John 19:1–3,16–18, The response to violence

_4_ FACING PAIN AND VIOLENCE

Aim: to consider how we cope with pain and violence when we experience or witness it.

WAY IN

Discuss with another member of the group any experience of pain or violence, whether physical or otherwise, which you have faced or witnessed (through television, for example). How did you react? Commit to prayer such issues as you feel appropriate.

Songs to sing
And can it be, SOF21, MP33, TS21.
For this purpose, SOF114, MP155, TS111.
From heaven you came, SOF120, MP162, TS114.
Hallelujah, my Father, SOF152, MP206.
Led like a lamb, SOF322, MP402, TS312.
O let the Son of God enfold you, SOF419, MP502, TS392.
O Love that will not let me go, SOF434, MP515.
O sacred head, once wounded, SOF446, MP520.
Ride on, ride on in majesty, SOF485, MP580.
There is a green hill far away, SOF542, MP674.

Music to listen to
Mendelssohn: Piano concerto no. 2 in D minor (Adagio), from *Adagio 2*.
'Beata lux', from *Libera*.
Enya: 'Pax deorum', from *The Memory of Trees*.

Read John 19:1–3, 16–18; The response to violence

Then Pilate took Jesus and had him flogged. And the soldiers wove a crown of thorns and put it on his head, and they dressed him in a purple robe. They kept coming up to him, saying, 'Hail, King of the Jews!' and striking him on the face...

Then he handed him over to them to be crucified.

So they took Jesus; and carrying the cross by himself, he went out to what is called The Place of the Skull, which in Hebrew is called Golgotha. There they crucified him, and with him two others, one on either side, with Jesus between them. Pilate also had an inscription written and put on the cross. It read, 'Jesus of Nazareth, the King of the Jews.'

Jesus' teaching was considered hard in his day (John 6:60–66); today, they are perhaps even more so. The language of society is, in many spheres of life, based on the language of conflict: for example, sport and politics are just two areas that are conducted using the atmosphere and analogy of warfare to excite interest. We may be urged to 'put the boot in first' or 'destroy the opposition'; to be told to turn the other cheek (Luke 6:29) seems very strange advice indeed. Yet Jesus would neither lead a revolution nor allow violence to be used in his defence: even as he was being arrested, he healed a man whose ear had been cut off during the fray (Luke 22:51).

At no time did Jesus respond to the violence and pain inflicted on him other than with dignity. Neither did he react to the taunting or verbal abuse he suffered, even from one of the thieves crucified with him. By his conduct, he shows us that the strength of love built up securely within us is the only basis that will sustain us through the hard times.

The perpetrators of great cruelty and oppression, and the regimes they build, cannot endure, because they lack the ability to love or respect those they seek to govern. It is, however, surprisingly easy for all authority to slip into actions or attitudes that are oppressive and lacking in compassion, and which inevitably lead to a painful outcome.

Discussion

It sometimes seems that violence, whether physical or verbal, is all around us. Individuals resort to violence all too quickly (road rage, football hooliganism). Religious and regional groupings as well as nations can also find violence hard to avoid. How do we react to violence or confrontation, whether physical or verbal? Do we find it difficult to exercise self-control in the face of this sort of behaviour?

As a group, think about and then discuss how we handle or react to conduct that produces or threatens pain or violence, whether to ourselves, to someone close to us, or when we encounter it at a distance (eg through the media).

LIFE

In dealing with an experience of pain or violent behaviour, what effect has it had on your relationship with...

Jesus?

people with whom you work or are in fellowship?

those to whom you are closest?

What have you discovered about yourself from that experience, and is there anything you need to do as a result?

RESPONSE

Discuss together any answers to the questions in the 'Life' section which have troubled, surprised or encouraged you. Pray for any individual or group of people recently subjected to painful or violent behaviour.

MEDITATION

Violence and pain

I live everywhere.
I have existed from the start,
since time began and humankind emerged.
I have taken my chances – it was the only way.
Sometimes I have prospered, but not often.

I am black in a white world,
white in a yellow world,
brown in a black world.
I am any colour and none,
any shade, any creed; anyone in minority.

continued >>>

I have been a Jew in Germany,
a Christian in Israel
a Muslim in Russia,
a Tibetan Buddhist in my own land.
I have been a small African tribe in a big country
mapped out by someone who knew nothing of my situation.

We are the children born of lust, anger and carelessness,
the misfits, the misshapen and unwanted.
We are those who do not conform to the pattern
the powerful define for us.
We are rejected, the abandoned, the neglected.
We are the refugees, the old and out-of-date.
We all suffer the violence and pain of the scapegoat.
You will find us in the gulag, the holocaust and the crossfire.
We are your conscience –
but do you hear us?

Praise

Leader:	The Servant of God suffered.
All:	**The Lord is the Light of life.**
Leader:	The Lord has borne our iniquity.
All:	**The Lord is the Light of life.**
Leader:	The Lord poured out his life.
All:	**And he is our salvation.**

(Based on Isaiah 53:11–12)

READINGS FOR THE WEEK

4 Facing pain and violence

Reflection	Day 5	1 Peter 1:18–23, The example of Jesus
	Day 6	Proverbs 3:29–35, Righteous living
	Day 7	John 16:12–22, Pain will turn to joy

5 Facing silence and desolation

Preparation	Day 1	Mark 14:53–61, The high priest faces the silence of Jesus
	Day 2	Luke 23:1–9, Herod faces the silence of Jesus
	Day 3	Acts 8:26–38, The power of the silent Lamb
◆ Meeting	Day 4	Matthew 27:11–14, Pilate faces silence

5 FACING SILENCE AND DESOLATION

Aim: to explore silence and feelings of desolation and how we deal with them, remembering how Jesus used silence and coped with desolation.

WAY IN

Have you ever had to confront silence or feelings of desolation, either personally or alongside someone else you care about? Discuss this with another member of your group for a few minutes, then pray about any issues raised.

Songs to sing
Come see the beauty of the Lord, SOF74, MP100.
Dear Lord and Father of mankind, SOF79, MP111, TS79.
I cannot tell, SOF205, MP266, TS199.
Immortal, Invisible, SOF234, MP327, TS220.
I will sing the wondrous story, SOF278, MP315.
Make me a channel of your peace, SOF381, MP456, TS348.
Praise you, Lord, SOF472, MP565.
River, wash over me, SOF487, MP581, TS441.
Rock of ages, SOF488, MP582.
You are my hiding place, SOF625, MP793.

Music to listen to
Bach: Toccata (Adagio and Fugue) BWV 564, from *Adagio 2*.
'Mysterium', from *Libera*.
Enya: 'La sonadora', from *The Memory of Trees*.

Read Matthew 27:11–14; Pilate faces silence

Now Jesus stood before the governor; and the governor asked him, 'Are you the King of the Jews?' Jesus said, 'You say so.' But when he was accused by the chief priests and elders, he did not answer. Then Pilate said to him, 'Do you not hear how many accusations they make against you?' But he gave him no answer, not even to a single charge, so that the governor was greatly amazed.

Jesus encountered silence in Gethsemane when the time came for him to face the beginning of his final trial. The disciples slept (Luke 22:45), so he faced alone the decision to be obedient and to die (Phil 2:8). But the soldiers who taunted and scourged him, Herod who questioned him and Pilate who was mystified by him all faced a silent response from Jesus. This kind of behaviour contrasts starkly with the sort of aggression we see today that often appears to be provoked by the most trivial of imagined insults: both road rage and air rage have produced extreme violence. Even looking at someone in what they consider 'the wrong way' can have consequences that far exceed the offence.

Neither Herod nor Pilate could understand why Jesus did not wish to plead for his life. They both offered him ways out of the situation: Herod suggested he might respond favourably to a few miracles; Pilate presented the Barabbas option. But they both failed to realise that now there was no turning back for Jesus, nothing that could be said or done to change his decision.

Then came his final cry of desolation as he died for us on the cross (Matt 27:46). This breaking of his silence was the moment in which Jesus faced his humanity. But his resources of loving obedience were able to bear the cruelty, disloyalty, pain and injustice inflicted on him by the world, and to overcome it.

Discussion

Facing open hostility with silence is hard; but facing silence can be difficult, too – the feelings of frustration may be overwhelming. As a group, think about this and discuss how you handle silence as individuals and as a church. Are you able to remain silent in the face of provocation?

LIFE

Sometimes those from whom we expect support let us down. At moments of crisis, we find ourselves alone or in a place where there seems to be nowhere to turn. Does the way in which Jesus dealt with his circumstances help you understand your own situation and cope with it better?

How have experiences of silence or desolation (whether from others or as your own response to a situation) affected your relationship with...

Jesus?

people with whom you work or are in fellowship?

those to whom you are closest?

What have you discovered about yourself from these experiences, and is there anything you need to do as a result?

RESPONSE

Discuss together any responses to the questions in the 'Life' section which have troubled, surprised or encouraged you. Pray for anyone facing silence or coping with feelings of desolation.

MEDITATION

Silence and desolation

There is a silence like the cloak of night
which wraps itself around us as we sleep.
It guards our thoughts and dreams while we're at rest
and gives protection as a castle's keep.

But silence, like the clouds, can change its role.
The sky can turn to darkness, sun to rain.
The silence shared by friends can alter too,
and loss of contact leads to heartfelt pain.

The garden anguish marked the changing scene
with friends asleep and opposition near.
The Father's absence, eloquently quiet,
the lonely vigil, counteracting fear.

The final desolation tears the air.
The veil is rent in holiness laid bare.

Praise

Leader:	The Lord has been silent.
All:	**The Lord is our refuge.**
Leader:	The Lord is to be feared.
All:	**The Lord is our refuge.**
Leader:	The Lord knows all our works.
All:	**Those who fear him will not perish.**

(Based on Isaiah 57:11–13)

READINGS FOR THE WEEK

5 Facing silence and desolation

Reflection	Day 5	Psalm 4:1–8, Trusting in the Lord
	Day 6	Ecclesiastes 3:1–8, The place of silence in life
	Day 7	Isaiah 53:1–12, A time for rejoicing

6 Facing the future

Preparation	Day 1	Romans 5:12–21, Living in grace
	Day 2	Romans 6:1–23, Slaves of righteousness
	Day 3	Hebrews 5:1–10, Obedience leading to salvation
◆ Meeting	Day 4	John 17:1–26, Jesus prays

<u>6</u> FACING THE FUTURE

Aim: to consider our attitude towards the challenge of the future.

WAY IN

Are you expecting to face a challenge in the future, either personally or alongside someone you care about? Discuss with another member of the group how you view this, then pray about the issues raised.

Songs to sing
Here I am, SOF167, MP229, TS161.
Jesus! The name high over all, SOF307, MP385, TS298.
O Jesus, I have promised, SOF418, MP501, TS391.
O Lord our God, SOF426, MP507, TS398.
O my Saviour, lifted, SOF437, MP516.
Restore, O Lord, SOF483, MP579, TS439.
Thank you for the cross, SOF522, MP632, TS473.
The price is paid, SOF540, MP663, TS487.
There is a Redeemer, SOF544, MP673, TS492.
When I survey the wondrous cross, SOF596, MP755, TS572.

Music to listen to
Mozart: Flute Concerto in G major (Adagio), from *Adagio 2*.
'Jubilate', from *Libera*.
Enya: 'Athair ar Neamh', from *The Memory of Trees*.

Read John 17:1–26; Jesus prays

After Jesus had spoken these words, he looked up to heaven and said, 'Father, the hour has come; glorify your Son so that the Son may glorify you, since you have given him authority over all people, to give eternal life to all whom you have given him. And this is eternal life, that they may know you, the only true God, and Jesus Christ whom you have sent. I glorified you on earth by finishing the work that you gave me to do. So now, Father, glorify me in your own presence with the glory that I had in your presence before the world existed.

'I have made your name known to those whom you gave me from the world. They were yours, and you gave them to me, and they have kept your word. Now they know that everything you have given me is from you; for the words that you gave to me I have given to them, and they have received them and know in truth that I came from you; and they have believed that you sent me. I am asking on their behalf; I am not asking on behalf of the world, but on behalf of those whom you gave me, because they are yours. All mine are yours, and yours are mine; and I have been glorified in them. And now I am no longer in the world, but they are in the world, and I am coming to you. Holy Father, protect them in your name that you have given me, so that they may be one, as we are one. While I was with them, I protected them in your name that you have given me. I guarded them, and not one of them was lost except the one destined to be lost, so that scripture might be fulfilled. But now I am coming to you, and I speak these things in the world so that they may have my joy made complete in themselves. I have given them your word, and the world has hated them because they do not belong to the world, just as I do not belong to the world. I am not asking you to take them out of the world, but I ask you to protect them from the evil one. They do not belong to the world, just as I do not belong to the world. Sanctify them in the truth; your word is truth. As you have sent me into the world, so I have sent them into the world. And for their sakes I sanctify myself, so that they also may be sanctified in truth.

'I ask not only on behalf of these, but also on behalf of those who will believe in me through their word, that they may all be one. As you, Father, are in me and I am in you, may they also be in us, so that the world may believe that you have sent me. The glory that you have given me I have given them, so that they may be one, as we are one, I in them and you in me, that they may become completely one, so that the world may know that you have sent me and have loved them even as you have loved me. Father, I desire that those also, whom you have given me, may be with me where I am, to see my glory, which you have given me because you loved me before the foundation of the world.

'Righteous Father, the world does not know you, but I know you; and these know that you have sent me. I made your name known to them, and I will make it known, so that the love with which you have loved me may be in them, and I in them.'

Following the Last Supper, as Jesus faced the final stage of his earthly journey, he prayed for himself, for his disciples and for all believers. It was the fulfilment of this prayer that sustained him and, in due course, his disciples; it is the fulfilment of this prayer that will carry us through the cross and into the future.

In Gethsemane, Jesus faced the days immediately ahead of him and prepared to meet the challenge of his humanity. Looking to the future beyond the cross would mean leaving this earth and rejoining his Father, but doing so as a human being and our representative. Facing the future when his journey began had meant Jesus, the man trusting God the Father of humankind, as we must all do. Facing the future beyond the cross meant Jesus, the Son of God, trusting us to follow his example by carrying on the work he had begun.

Jesus prays that we will be in him as he is in his Father, and commits himself to dwell in those who believe in him as the Father dwells in him (John 17:23). This will give us the protection we need as we face the challenge of the future and take the love of Jesus out into the world. As our personal commitment to Jesus deepens and we share his response to us with the people we encounter, we will find ourselves growing in spiritual maturity and changing as individuals.

Discussion
The growth and change Jesus encourages us to undertake personally are echoed by the growth and change going on around us all the time in the world. The problem for us is that the world's objectives are very different. We are called to keep our eyes fixed on Jesus; however, the world's focus is very much on economic and material values.

As a group, consider and then discuss how you might cope with the future in the face of this conflict of interests. In particular, how might you improve the balance between the spiritual and the secular spheres of your life?

LIFE

When you think about the challenge of the future, have you discovered anything about yourself or those around you which you have found difficult to cope with or which has been an encouragement (or both)?

How could this affect your relationship with...

1) Jesus?

2) people with whom you work or are in fellowship?

3) those to whom you are closest?

4) What have you discovered about yourself from that experience, and is there anything you need to do as a result?

RESPONSE

Discuss together any responses to the questions in the 'Life' section which have troubled, surprised or encouraged you. Pray for each other as you face the uncertainty of the world's direction in the future. Use this time as an opportunity to reaffirm your commitment to Jesus.

MEDITATION

Facing the future (Mary)

It seems to have come and gone so quickly –
this life that was entrusted to my body thirty or so years ago.
From those early days of uncertainty, when Joseph wavered,
through to the desolation of Golgotha,
then the joy of reunion and the coming of the Spirit –
it's all so bewildering.

I should be devastated by the death of my eldest son,
but how can I be?
Jesus is alive.
They saw him taken up to heaven.

He has left me with another task,
in addition to all my other children and grandchildren –
to keep house and look after John.
I can't go out teaching, like the others
but I can guard what I know, what I've seen,
what I've thought about over the years.
I can share it with John.
Perhaps he'll do something with it all.
Maybe he'll write it down,
like some of the others are doing –
young Mark, for instance.

The challenge is to see the future,
not live in the past;
to live out what we know,
not dwell on the 'might have beens'.
I've been given someone to believe in
and a treasure to share in what I have learned and felt –
and it is enough.

Praise

Leader:	When we call, the Lord will answer.
All:	**His light shall break forth like the dawn.**
Leader:	The Lord will go before us.
All:	**His glory will be our rear guard.**
Leader:	When we cry for help.
All:	**He will say, 'Here am I.'**

(Based on Isaiah 58:8–9)

READINGS FOR THE WEEK

6 Facing the future

Reflection	Day 5	1 John 1:1–10, Cleansed from unrighteousness
	Day 6	1 John 2:1–17, Do not love the world
	Day 7	1 John 2:18–29, Abide in Jesus

OTHER RESOURCES FROM SCRIPTURE UNION

Closer to God
Reading the Bible in the power of the Holy Spirit
ISSN 1362-914X, £2.50 per quarter.
Quarterly notes with a creative and reflective approach and an emphasis on renewal. There is a Bible reading with notes for every day of the week, together with 'going deeper' meditations, special features and theme weeks.

Sitting at the Feet of Jesus
Stephen and Jacalyn Eyre
ISBN 1 85999 020 7, £3.50
This Spiritual Encounter Guide on the Sermon on the Mount offers a fresh approach to personal devotion for new or long-time Christians. The aim of these Bible studies is to help readers find intimacy with God. The book contains one month's Bible reading material.

Through the Bible in a Year: A spiritual journal
Dennis Lennon
ISBN 1 85999 196 3, £9.99
A new syllabus constructed around eleven themes, gives an overarching picture of the whole Bible story. There is space for the reader to keep a written record of their spiritual journey.

Ready to Grow: Practical steps to knowing God better
Alan Harkness
ISBN 0 949720 71 2, £5.99
An attractive yet practical book to encourage believers to make time with God a regular part of their lives. Includes chapters on preparation, getting started, the practicalities, sharing what you have learned, and different methods of combining Bible reading and prayer.

Feet on the Ground
Peta Sherlock and John Lane
ISBN 0 949720 61 5, £1.50
These fifteen Bible readings, with notes and guides for medi-
tation, are ideal for personal retreat at Advent, Christmas or
any time of the year, and for those preparing for mission. The
booklet includes questions and topics for group discussion.
Previous experience in daily devotions is not necessary.

How to Read the Bible for All its Worth (2nd edition)
Gordon D Fee and Douglas Stewart
ISBN 0 86201 974 5, £7.50
This in-depth Bible reading guide is consistently popular and
fast becoming a classic. 'If we want to get the most out of the
psalms or the parables of Jesus, or the letters of Paul, how can
we distinguish what is of abiding relevance from what is
purely local and temporary? ... I do not remember reading any
other book which gave so much help in the answering of these
questions as this one does.' *F F Bruce, Late Emeritus
Professor of Biblical Criticism and Exegesis, University of
Manchester.*